STUDY GUIDE

PROPHETIC IDENTITY *and* DESTINY

Copyright © 2025 by Tim Bagwell

Published by AVAIL

All rights reserved. No portion of this book may be reproduced, stored in a retrieval system, or transmitted in any form or by any means—electronic, mechanical, photocopy, recording, scanning, or other—except for brief quotations in critical reviews or articles, without prior written permission of the author.

Unless otherwise noted, all Scripture quotations are taken from the New King James Version®. Copyright © 1982 by Thomas Nelson. Used by permission. All rights reserved. | Scripture quotations marked KJV are taken from the King James Version of the Bible. Public domain.

For foreign and subsidiary rights, contact the author.

Cover design by: Sara Young
Cover photo by: Monty Nuss

ISBN: 978-1-964794-68-6   1 2 3 4 5 6 7 8 9 10

Printed in the United States of America

STUDY GUIDE

PROPHETIC IDENTITY *and* DESTINY

TIM BAGWELL

AVAIL

CONTENTS

INTRODUCTION...6

PART 1   PROPHETIC PROMISE AND THE BLOOD......13

Chapter 1.   THE PROMISE AND THE PROBLEM 14
Chapter 2.   THE KEYS TO POSSESSION 20
Chapter 3.   POWER OF THE BLOOD 26

PART 2   EMPOWERED FOR THE PROMISE 33

Chapter 4.   POWER OF THE DREAM............................34
Chapter 5.   THE POWER OF VIRTUE 40
Chapter 6.   POWER TO ENDURE 46
Chapter 7.   POWER TO PROSPER 52

PART 3   READY TO REIGN......................................59

Chapter 8.   EMPOWERED FOR THE CALL 60
Chapter 9.   THE *KAIROS* MOMENT..............................66
Chapter 10.   AUTHORITY TO REIGN 72

Foreword by Samuel Rodriguez

PROPHETIC IDENTITY and DESTINY

YOU ARE **WHO GOD SAYS** YOU ARE

TIM BAGWELL

INTRODUCTION

God is not a predictor; He is a Creator.

READING TIME

As you read the Introduction in ***Prophetic Identity and Destiny***, reflect on, and respond to the text by answering the following questions.

REVIEW, REFLECT, AND RESPOND:

In your own words, what does it mean to define one's future by what God has said? Pro-vide a practical example from your own life.

_____
_____
_____
_____
_____
_____

We must choose between a historically limited vision and a prophetic one. Which perspec-tive do you currently lead from—and how do you know?

_____
_____
_____
_____
_____
_____

> *"Where there is no vision, the people perish: but he that keepeth the law, happy is he."*
>
> **—Proverbs 29:18 (KJV)**

Consider the scripture above and answer the following questions:

In what areas of your life have you operated without prophetic vision—and what has been the result?

_____
_____
_____
_____
_____
_____
_____

What does "perishing" look like in your personal life or leadership when you're not operating with a clear, God-given vision? Provide an example.

_____
_____
_____
_____
_____
_____
_____
_____

When might you have unknowingly allowed the darkness, void, or chaos of your past to dictate what you believe God could do in your future?

_____
_____
_____
_____
_____
_____
_____
_____
_____

The introduction compares Joseph's prophetic dreams to the church's current need for divine guid-ance. What are the "dreams" or promises God has spoken to you personally, and how are you stewarding them?

_____
_____
_____
_____
_____
_____
_____
_____
_____

How often do you find yourself trying to "understand" your calling through a natural lens rather than seeking spiritual insight?

_____
_____
_____
_____
_____
_____
_____

When was the last time you allowed your history—failures, disappointments, or missed opportuni-ties—to determine your level of faith or ambition?

_____
_____
_____
_____
_____
_____
_____
_____

In what areas might you have compromised your prophetic edge in favor of security or social ac-ceptance?

_____
_____
_____

Anointed eyesight sees from afar. Who in your life helps you lift your perspective to see propheti-cally rather than reactively?

What is the current cost of your prophetic vision? Are you willing to pay it—or have you resisted the discomfort it requires?

PART 1

PROPHETIC PROMISE AND THE BLOOD

CHAPTER 1

THE PROMISE AND THE PROBLEM

Compromise and the anointing are incompatible.

READING TIME

As you read Chapter 1: "The Promise and the Problem" in *Prophetic Identity and Destiny*, reflect on, and respond to the text by answering the following questions.

REVIEW, REFLECT, AND RESPOND:

This chapter contrasts passive survivors with active possessors. In your own life or leader-ship, where have you settled for survival instead of stepping into spiritual authority?

_____
_____
_____
_____
_____
_____
_____

What "giants" have intimidated you out of trusting God's promise—and what would it look like to fight for that territory instead?

_____
_____
_____
_____
_____
_____
_____

> *"Every place that the sole of your foot will tread upon I have given you, as I said to Moses."*
>
> —**Joshua 1:3**

Consider the scripture above and answer the following questions:

What promises has God already given you that you've yet to "tread upon"? What is holding you back from taking that first step?

_____
_____
_____
_____
_____
_____
_____

In what ways can your faith be expressed practically this week to take the territory God has de-clared as yours?

_____
_____
_____
_____
_____
_____
_____

Where have you allowed a "maintenance mindset" to replace your hunger for prophetic movement and breakthrough?

_____
_____
_____
_____
_____
_____

What patterns of compromise have crept into your habits, thoughts, or leadership that are incompat-ible with the anointing you carry?

_____
_____
_____
_____
_____
_____

Think about your team or organization: what signs indicate whether you're living in provision or truly moving toward possession?

_____
_____
_____
_____
_____
_____

Caleb saw the same giants as the other spies but filtered his view through the promise of God. What lens are you using to evaluate challenges in your life and calling?

_____
_____
_____
_____
_____
_____
_____
_____

"The less willing you are to fight, the less there is to win." What spiritual battles have you avoided out of fear, weariness, or intimidation?

_____
_____
_____
_____
_____
_____
_____
_____

What are the "kings" (strongholds, addictions, fears, false identities) that still rule in territory God has promised you—and what action plan will you take to confront them?

_____
_____

When was the last time you saw yourself as a grasshopper instead of a giant-slayer? What truth from God's Word needs to be reestablished in your identity?

Are you fighting for your inheritance—your family, calling, territory—or are you camped out on the wrong side of the Jordan waiting for God to act first?

CHAPTER 2

THE KEYS TO POSSESSION

*"God never inhabits people's pitifulness.
He inhabits their praises."*

READING TIME

As you read Chapter 2: "The Keys to Possession" in
Prophetic Identity and Destiny, reflect on, and respond
to the text by answering the following questions.

REVIEW, REFLECT, AND RESPOND:

"The only warfare that counts is spiritual." What battles have you been fighting in the flesh that require spiritual weapons?

_____
_____
_____
_____
_____
_____
_____

Judah's victory came through obedience and praise. What would change if your first response in spiritual battles was worship instead of worry?

_____
_____
_____
_____
_____
_____
_____

> *"Have I not commanded you? Be strong and of good courage; do not be afraid, nor be dismayed, for the LORD your God is with you wherever you go."*
>
> *—Joshua 1:9*

Consider the scripture above and answer the following questions:

What specific situation are you facing where fear or dismay is tempting you to forget that God is with you?

_____
_____
_____
_____
_____
_____
_____
_____

How can you practice courage this week—not just emotionally, but as a spiritual obedience to God's command?

_____
_____
_____
_____
_____
_____
_____
_____

In what areas of your life are you asleep to the reality of spiritual warfare—and how has that left your leadership or family vulnerable?

_____
_____
_____
_____
_____
_____

What "false sense of security" have you allowed to form while the enemy has been steadily advancing?

_____
_____
_____
_____
_____
_____

What does your response to battles usually look like? Do you lean more on strategy and reaction or obedience and praise?

_____
_____
_____
_____
_____
_____

Have you ever faced a "Jehoshaphat moment"—a battle where you were told to stand still? How did you respond, and what was the outcome?

_____
_____
_____
_____
_____
_____
_____
_____

Which lies about your identity still influence how you think about your authority, calling, or leadership? What truth from God's Word needs to be reestablished?

_____
_____
_____
_____
_____
_____
_____
_____

"Victory is a choice." What choices have you been avoiding that are keeping you from your promised land?

_____
_____
_____

Are there outdated ways God provided in the past (your "manna") that you are still clinging to instead of stepping into new blessings?

What will your next "memorial stone" be—a marker of God's faithfulness that you need to intentionally build to stir your faith and legacy?

CHAPTER 3

POWER OF THE BLOOD

"If His blood does not flow through us, we are nothing, and we can do nothing."

READING TIME

As you read Chapter 3: "Power of the Blood" in *Prophetic Identity and Destiny*, reflect on, and respond to the text by answering the following questions.

REVIEW, REFLECT, AND RESPOND:

We can perpetually live beneath our birthright if we don't grasp the reality of Jesus's blood. In what ways have you neglected or minimized the power of the blood in your own walk with God?

___
___
___
___
___
___
___

The prodigal son "came to himself" in the pigpen. What personal or leadership moment has served as your wake-up call—and how did the blood of Jesus lead you out?

___
___
___
___
___
___
___

> *"You were not redeemed with corruptible things, like silver and gold, from your aimless conduct received by tradition from your fathers, but with the precious blood of Christ, as of a lamb without blemish and without spot."*
>
> **—1 Peter 1:18-19**

Consider the scripture above and answer the following questions:

What "corruptible things" or traditions have you relied on instead of fully trusting in the power of Jesus's blood?

_____
_____
_____
_____
_____
_____
_____

How does the phrase "precious blood of Christ" challenge you to reframe your understanding of salvation, covenant, and spiritual authority?

_____
_____
_____
_____
_____
_____
_____
_____

When was the last time you pleaded the blood of Jesus over your mind, your decisions, or your leadership responsibilities? What difference did it make?

_____
_____
_____
_____
_____
_____

Have you treated the concept of the blood as a spiritual cliché instead of a living, covenantal reality? If so, what needs to shift?

_____
_____
_____
_____
_____
_____

What areas of your life—past wounds, spiritual battles, emotional trauma—still need the cleansing, protective, and restoring work of the blood?

_____
_____
_____
_____
_____
_____
_____

"The blood of sprinkling speaks better things." What is your life testifying to right now—judgment and striving or mercy and restoration?

___

Are you applying the blood to the "doorposts" of your heart daily or only in times of crisis? How so?

___

In what ways is your spiritual immune system weak—and what practices could strengthen your reliance on Jesus's blood and the Spirit's power?

___

The chapter makes it clear: you can't live victoriously off someone else's prayers. Where have you outsourced your spiritual strength, and how can you reclaim it?

What would change in your leadership, family, and decision-making if you lived fully convinced that "the blood covers every area of your life"?

PART 2

EMPOWERED FOR THE PROMISE

CHAPTER 4

POWER OF THE DREAM

"People who are willing to pay a price for their anointing will be misunderstood."

READING TIME

As you read Chapter 4: "Power of the Dream" in *Prophetic Identity and Destiny*, reflect on, and respond to the text by answering the following questions.

REVIEW, REFLECT, AND RESPOND:

Joseph "kept himself, year after year." In the face of persecution, misunderstanding, and loss, are you still keeping yourself? How do you know?

___

Joseph refused to let his brothers' bitterness smother his anointing. What voices have tried to silence or distort your God-given dream—and how have you responded?

___

> *"Now Joseph had a dream, and he told it to his brothers; and they hated him even more."*
>
> **—Genesis 37:5**

Consider the scripture above and answer the following questions:

Why do you think sharing your God-given vision often invites resistance, even from those close to you?

_____
_____
_____
_____
_____
_____
_____
_____

How do you discern when to share a dream—and when to quietly steward it?

_____
_____
_____
_____
_____
_____
_____
_____

Have you ever been punished for doing the right thing, like Joseph was? How did that experience shape your spiritual posture?

_____
_____
_____
_____
_____
_____
_____

What dream has God placed in your heart that's been tested by betrayal, delay, or confusion—and how have you guarded it?

_____
_____
_____
_____
_____
_____
_____

In what areas have you been tempted to downplay your anointing or spiritual gifts in order to maintain peace or avoid rejection?

_____
_____
_____
_____
_____
_____
_____

Are there generational callings or heritage-level blessings in your life—your "coat of many colors"—that you've neglected or hidden?

_____
_____
_____
_____
_____
_____
_____
_____

What's your response when people misjudge your motives? Do you react with self-pity and withdrawal or with endurance and integrity like Joseph?

_____
_____
_____
_____
_____
_____
_____
_____

Have you ever been called prideful or arrogant for simply believing what God said about you? How can you discern the difference between pride and prophetic confidence?

_____
_____

"Without a prophetic dream, an anointed, empowered lifestyle cannot develop." What vision is fueling your life and leadership right now?

Have you ever mistaken external success for spiritual favor? How does Joseph's journey redefine what it means to be favored by God?

CHAPTER 5

THE POWER OF VIRTUE

"Righteousness and pride don't mix."

READING TIME

As you read Chapter 5: "The Power of Virtue" in *Prophetic Identity and Destiny*, reflect on, and respond to the text by answering the following questions.

REVIEW, REFLECT, AND RESPOND:

Joseph chose to suffer his brothers' wrath rather than compromise his integrity. Where in your life have you been tempted to exchange holiness for approval?

_____
_____
_____
_____
_____
_____
_____

Joseph's virtue led to betrayal, not applause. Are you willing to remain upright even when righteousness costs you your comfort, position, or relationships? Describe a time when you chose to honor God even though it cost you something valuable.

_____
_____
_____
_____
_____
_____
_____

> *"As for me, You uphold me in my integrity,*
> *and set me before Your face forever."*
>
> **—Psalm 41:12**

Consider the scripture above and answer the following questions:

What does it mean to be upheld by God because of your integrity—and where in your life do you need God to be your upholder right now?

_____
_____
_____
_____
_____
_____
_____

In light of this verse, what areas of your heart, habits, or leadership still need to come into alignment with God's standard of integrity?

_____
_____
_____
_____
_____
_____
_____

Joseph didn't just avoid sin; he cultivated holiness. What practices or habits in your life reflect not just avoidance of sin, but pursuit of righteousness?

_____
_____
_____
_____
_____
_____

Virtue requires "swimming against the tide." Where are you currently being called to stand alone—and what fear is holding you back?

_____
_____
_____
_____
_____
_____

Joseph rejected Potiphar's wife, not just for his own sake, but to honor God and others. What decisions do you need to make to protect the future God has entrusted to you?

_____
_____
_____
_____
_____
_____

In seasons of betrayal or misunderstanding, have you retaliated or rested in God's role as Defender? Provide an example. What would it look like to fully trust Him with justice?

___

Joseph lived with excellence in obscurity before he was trusted with leadership. How are you stewarding your current "hidden" season?

___

Have you confused charisma for character in yourself or others? How has that affected your discernment or leadership decisions?

___

Where in your life has success or favor tempted you to loosen your spiritual convictions—and what does it mean to "walk securely" again?

Are you training your children, team, or community to prioritize holiness and integrity, even when no one's watching? How so?

CHAPTER 6

POWER TO ENDURE

"God's strategic opportunities come after His divine delays, not before."

READING TIME

As you read Chapter 6: "Power to Endure" in ***Prophetic Identity and Destiny***, reflect on, and respond to the text by answering the following questions.

REVIEW, REFLECT, AND RESPOND:

Joseph's "wondering did not lead to wandering." When your life feels delayed or misaligned with God's promises, do you tend to wait with God or wander away from Him?

_____
_____
_____
_____
_____
_____
_____

How do you respond when someone forgets to advocate for you, as the butler did with Joseph? Does disappointment derail your faith or deepen it?

_____
_____
_____
_____
_____
_____
_____

> *"Blessed is the man who endures temptation; for when he has been approved, he will receive the crown of life which the Lord has promised to those who love Him."*
>
> —James 1:12

Consider the scripture above and answer the following questions:

What trials are currently testing your endurance, and how can you embrace the promise of a "crown of life" as your motivation?

_____
_____
_____
_____
_____
_____
_____
_____

In what ways have you allowed impatience, offense, or discouragement to interfere with the perfecting work of endurance?

_____
_____
_____
_____
_____
_____
_____
_____

Have you confused inactivity with endurance? What does it look like to actively wait on God with excellence as Joseph did?

___

Where in your life do you need to stop second-guessing God's timing and start cooperating with His delays?

___

Joseph made every moment count—even in prison. How are you stewarding your current "waiting room" season?

___

Are there people you're still holding responsible for your setbacks—people God may be using to position you for destiny?

_____
_____
_____
_____
_____
_____
_____
_____
_____

When has impatience led you to force open a door that God didn't open yet? What was the result?

_____
_____
_____
_____
_____
_____
_____
_____
_____

How has your view of delay changed after seeing how Joseph's divine delays were part of his preparation and promotion?

_____
_____

"Enduring is one of the greatest keys to living an anointed lifestyle." How have you minimized endurance—and what spiritual disciplines do you need to re-engage?

If someone looked at your current attitude in hardship, what would they believe about your trust in God's plan?

CHAPTER 7

POWER TO PROSPER

"You just need to know that you are who God says you are—and whatever He says is yours is yours."

READING TIME

As you read Chapter 7: "Power to Prosper" in *Prophetic Identity and Destiny*, reflect on, and respond to the text by answering the following questions.

REVIEW, REFLECT, AND RESPOND:

Joseph "prospered in the places that were supposed to destroy him." Are there circumstances in your life right now where God may be asking you to do the same?

_____
_____
_____
_____
_____
_____
_____

Joseph never asked, "What's in it for me?" In what areas have self-interest or comparison poisoned your ability to trust God's process?

_____
_____
_____
_____
_____
_____
_____

> *"As for every man to whom God has given riches and wealth, and given him power to eat of it, to receive his heritage and rejoice in his labor—this is the gift of God."*
>
> **—Ecclesiastes 5:19**

Consider the scripture above and answer the following questions:

In what ways are you resisting or receiving the "gift of God" that includes rejoicing in your labor?

_____
_____
_____
_____
_____
_____
_____
_____

What would change in your mindset if you began to see prosperity not as a destination but as a gift already working in your current obedience?

_____
_____
_____
_____
_____
_____
_____
_____

When someone else's success triggers your insecurity, do you see it as a threat—or a reminder of God's ability to bless in unexpected places? Describe the most recent example.

_____
_____
_____
_____
_____
_____

Where are you currently planted that feels more like Egypt than promise—and how are you making yourself useful and faithful anyway?

_____
_____
_____
_____
_____
_____

What natural "lack" do you focus on that may be distracting you from the spiritual riches God already deposited in you?

_____
_____
_____
_____
_____
_____

What role has favor played in your leadership journey so far—and how have you stewarded it?

_____
_____
_____
_____
_____
_____
_____
_____

How has the "What's in it for me?" mindset held you back from God's best—and how can you break it?

_____
_____
_____
_____
_____
_____
_____
_____

Are you living with a poverty mindset that expects hardship more than favor? How is that shaping your speech, decisions, or leadership?

_____
_____
_____

How do you typically respond when someone recognizes your anointing—do you embrace it, deflect it, or hide from it? Why?

Have you been waiting for a new opportunity instead of fully honoring and excelling in the opportunity already in front of you?

PART 3

READY TO REIGN

CHAPTER 8

EMPOWERED FOR THE CALL

"The call and the power are like twins in the womb: they are always together."

READING TIME

As you read Chapter 8: "Empowered for the Call" in *Prophetic Identity and Destiny*, reflect on, and respond to the text by answering the following questions.

REVIEW, REFLECT, AND RESPOND:

"If He calls you, He gifts you. If He gifts you, He empowers you." Have you believed the calling but doubted the power? Where has that led to striving or burnout?

_____
_____
_____
_____
_____
_____
_____

Are you pursuing something God never called you to—or failing to walk in the power He already gave you for something He did?

_____
_____
_____
_____
_____
_____
_____

> *"For the gifts and the calling of God are irrevocable."*
>
> **—Romans 11:29**

Consider the scripture above and answer the following questions:

In what ways have you questioned or resisted God's irrevocable call on your life—and what do you need to surrender to fully embrace it?

_____

_____

_____

_____

_____

_____

_____

_____

How does knowing that God's calling cannot be revoked challenge your current mindset, excuses, or inaction?

_____

_____

_____

_____

_____

_____

_____

_____

This chapter describes enchrio and epichrio—anointing within and anointing upon. Which of these two have you cultivated more, and which one needs your attention?

What have you done recently to cultivate the enchrio—the internal anointing that shapes your character, mindset, and intimacy with God?

Where have you seen the epichrio—God's anointing upon you for others—at work in your life? How are you intentionally stepping into it more boldly?

Are you focused on sensation or assignment? What does your answer reveal about your understanding of the purpose of the anointing?

What would it look like to live as if your proclamation required a supernatural demonstration every day—in your home, your workplace, or your ministry?

In what areas have you relied on talent or training instead of the anointing—and what's been the result?

How are you stewarding the "anointing of preparation" right now? Are you resisting the refining season or embracing it?

_____
_____
_____
_____
_____
_____

Joseph's power to prosper was not just for himself—it blessed everyone around him. How are you using your anointing to break yokes and lift burdens for others?

_____
_____
_____
_____
_____
_____

Do you sense you're living in the anointing of revelation, preparation, or destination? How is God meeting you in this phase, and how are you responding?

_____
_____
_____
_____
_____
_____

CHAPTER 9

THE *KAIROS* MOMENT

"Kairos is more than a moment in chronological time; it is a moment in God's ordained timing."

READING TIME

As you read Chapter 9: "The *Kairos* Moment" in ***Prophetic Identity and Destiny***, reflect on, and respond to the text by answering the following questions.

REVIEW, REFLECT, AND RESPOND:

Kairos is a divine intersection of opportunity and purpose. Are you living in a way that's ready for your *kairos* moment—or are you distracted, discouraged, or disengaged?

_____
_____
_____
_____
_____
_____
_____

Joseph stood before Pharaoh not to gain favor but to serve a purpose. What's your motivation in moments of visibility—elevation or obedience?

_____
_____
_____
_____
_____
_____
_____

> *"And let us not grow weary while doing good, for in due season we shall reap if we do not lose heart."*
>
> —**Galatians 6:9**

Consider the scripture above and answer the following questions:

Where are you growing weary in well-doing—and what would it look like to renew your focus and faith for the "due season" ahead?

_____
_____
_____
_____
_____
_____
_____

Describe a moment when your obedience and endurance through difficulty finally produced visible fruit. What harvest might be waiting on the other side of your persistence now?

_____
_____
_____
_____
_____
_____
_____

Joseph shaved, changed clothes, and stepped into purpose in a single day—but he spent years getting ready. What has your "getting ready" season looked like?

_____
_____
_____
_____
_____
_____

How are you responding to closed doors, and what will you do in the meantime to prepare for them to open?

_____
_____
_____
_____
_____
_____

What systems, routines, or spiritual disciplines in your life are actively preparing you for a future you haven't yet seen?

_____
_____
_____
_____
_____
_____

When was the last time you stepped out in faith before the opportunity looked secure? What did that reveal about your trust in God's timing?

_____
_____
_____
_____
_____
_____
_____
_____

How has bitterness, disappointment, or self-pity threatened to disqualify you from your destiny garment?

_____
_____
_____
_____
_____
_____
_____
_____

What "old garments" are you still wearing that need to be left behind so you can be clothed for your next assignment?

_____
_____
_____
_____

Pharaoh gave Joseph his ring, robe, and authority. If God elevated you today, are there areas of unresolved pride, fear, or insecurity that would compromise your stewardship?

If your *kairos* moment came today, what would it find you doing? How does that answer convict, comfort, or challenge you?

CHAPTER 10

AUTHORITY TO REIGN

"When your heart is pure, God can cause you to flourish in the most imposing and unlikely places."

READING TIME

As you read Chapter 10: "Authority to Reign" in ***Prophetic Identity and Destiny***, reflect on, and respond to the text by answering the following questions.

REVIEW, REFLECT, AND RESPOND:

Power is not the same thing as authority. How do you know when you are functioning in power versus authority? Are you exercising one but not the other? Explain.

_____
_____
_____
_____
_____
_____
_____

Joseph refused to shrink back from influence, even in intimidating spaces. What doors has God opened for you that you've hesitated to walk through because of fear, insecurity, or imposter syndrome?

_____
_____
_____
_____
_____
_____
_____

> *"And I will give you the keys of the kingdom of heaven, and whatever you bind on earth will be bound in heaven, and whatever you loose on earth will be loosed in heaven."*
>
> **—Matthew 16:19**

Consider the scripture above and answer the following questions:

What have you tolerated in your life, family, or ministry that God has actually given you authority to bind or resist? Why?

_____
_____
_____
_____
_____
_____
_____
_____

What spiritual atmosphere are you creating in your home, workplace, or church with the words and authority you release?

_____
_____
_____
_____
_____
_____
_____
_____

What signs in your life indicate that you've been given authority—and how have you responded to that responsibility?

___

Joseph didn't leverage Pharaoh's fear for personal gain. Where are you tempted to use spiritual influence for self-promotion instead of service?

___

Are you asking God to entrust you with more, even while neglecting the territory He's already assigned to your care?

___

Have you mistaken fearlessness for faith—or delayed obedience because you wanted "more clarity"? What is God asking you to act on now?

___

When was the last time someone recognized God's presence or anointing in you without you saying a word, and what did you do with it?

___

How does your private character reflect your readiness for public authority?

___

In what ways has this book helped you better understand or define the prophetic promise God has spoken over your life?

What three specific actions or changes do you feel led to implement in your life after reading this book?

www.ingramcontent.com/pod-product-compliance
Lightning Source LLC
Chambersburg PA
CBHW062120080426
42734CB00012B/2935